Captured
by Love

...and raising a
generation captivated by God

KATIE MCHARGUE

Cover photo taken by Katie McHargue

FIRST EDITION

ISBN: 978-1-946466-14-3

Library of Congress Control Number: 2017938710

Published by

P.O. Box 2839, Apopka, FL 32704

Printed in the United States of America

Dedication

To my dear friend, LaDonna No Neck, who is courageously living passionately for Jesus on the Pine Ridge Reservation in South Dakota. I have learned so much from you about being a servant leader. Your beautiful heart, not only for your own five children but for so many of the hurting young people within the Lakota tribe, has inspired me and strengthened my faith. Thank you! I humbly dedicate this book to you. May your children grow to be the laid-down lovers of God and warriors they were created to be.

Introduction

I want to start by saying absolutely anything and everything in me that is good has been because of my glorious Lord and Savior Jesus Christ, who in His great mercy saved me and has been so gracious over the many, many years of walking with Him to free me, heal me, and constantly reveal Himself to me. I would not want to live a single moment without Jesus; for He is life to me!

Table of Contents

"*Older women likewise are to be reverent in behavior, not slanderers or slaves to much wine. They are to teach what is good, and so train the young women to love their husbands and children, to be self-controlled, pure, working at home, kind, and submissive to their own husbands, that the word of God may not be reviled.*"

(Titus 2:3-5)

"*Then Jesus declared, 'I am the Bread of Life. Whoever comes to me will never go hungry, and whoever believes in me will never be thirsty.'*"

(John 6:35)

"*Then the lord said to Moses, 'Behold, I will rain bread from heaven for you; and the people shall go out and gather a day's portion every day, that I may test them, whether or not they will walk in My instruction.'*"
(Exodus 16:4)

CHAPTER 1

The Day I Married Jesus

I was a freshman at the University of Cincinnati sometime in the spring semester the day I once and for all, for better or for worse, decided I was truly the bride of Christ…and it was one of the most difficult times of my life up until this point.

The walls of the musty basement of Smith Residence Hall were a depressing, concrete color. To be honest, I can't really remember anything cheerful about the atmosphere in our resident laundry room. With four quarters, I could do my wash. I remember hauling as much as I could carry down those nine flights of stairs, all the while feeling tightness in my chest and an ache in my nineteen-year-old heart that had just been broken. I wanted to be alone for a good cry, and I reasoned the dark, semi-moist, laundry room would be just the place on that otherwise beautiful, spring day. As soon as I laid my dirty clothes all over the cold, concrete floor to be sorted, the floodgates of my heart and eyeballs opened. I began to sob my heart out. You see, throughout most of high school and my first year of college, I had dated a very dear, young Christian man from a wonderful family, and I had, unfortunately, given my heart to him.

He and I had many years of good memories together and part of me had wondered if maybe this was the man I would marry. My parents had not raised me to understand what courtship to marriage looked like and encouraged me to date young...too young in my opinion, but hindsight provided wisdom too late.

Three months prior, my boyfriend had telephoned that the young lady he went on a blind date with (I had agreed to let him go on as a favor to a Christian friend) was the woman he was going to marry. For them, it had been love at first sight! Although I am so grateful to God for that now, you can imagine what it was like to hear that news after years of being together. God was very, very patient and good to me because I had been wrestling in my spirit for a while about this relationship knowing I was called by God to be a missionary in Africa...and my young boyfriend was feeling led to be a lawyer. We went back and forth. I was always hoping it would work out somehow until the day he met his dear wife. And bam! Just like that it was over.

That fateful morning in the laundry room happened to be his wedding day. He had a very short engagement! I had been invited to attend the wedding. A very kind, albeit strange gesture, but I declined and chose instead to bawl my eyes out. I still had feelings for this man, and felt I needed to get my act together and quick! God clearly had different plans for me and so I was crying out to Him to help me to get over it!

I bent over the top-loading washing machine while the tears spilled out of my eyes as my heart was literally feeling broken. All of a sudden I heard the voice of God. "Look down," the voice commanded. I wiped my eyes and looked down incredulously into that empty washer. Instantly, my eyes noticed something bright and shiny.... a beautiful, rose gold ring with the most interesting, decorative pattern of circles and small points all around. It fit my ring finger perfectly. In my spirit leapt the verse from Isaiah 54:4, "For your Maker is your Husband – the Lord Almighty is His name." I knew it was God speaking to me again. "Katie, just love Me. Just focus on Me and cultivate your love relationship with Me. I promise you when the time is right, I will give you a husband who will blow your mind!"

I looked at the lovely ring on my finger and doubted for just a smidgen maybe some dear girl doing laundry had lost it. It looked very valuable and so new. So, I resolved to report it to the dorm parent for any inquiries. I did and nothing ever came of it. The ring is still on my finger to this day—my wedding ring from Jesus! Two pieces of jewelry I almost never take off are my wedding ring from Jesus and my wedding ring from Wade. The two greatest loves in my life!

For several months, my mentor Heather had been trying to teach me about the incredible love God had for me and many times had emphasized I was His bride, the one He had chosen to be with forever. I had received prayer and participated in Bible studies for years, but I can tell you after that day in the laundry room my love relationship with Jesus changed and became my obsession. My gaze turned to Him for everything, and I completely looked at Him as my Husband. At night as I would drift off to sleep, often if not daily, I would run down a list of all the ways God had been such a wonderful Husband to me throughout the day. I would thank Him for providing and caring for me, protecting and loving me, speaking to me, and whatever else I could think of. I began to go on "dates" with Jesus. I even went as far as to dress up for Him, wear perfume, and go out with Him. I was able to spend time just loving Him and spending time together. (All the while of course recognizing His absolute holiness.) My dates were like extra-special, quiet times set aside for seeking Him and being with Him. I grew to love God so much. He satisfied my heart in such a deep way while I always knew one day I would marry. I was in no rush for that to happen.

That period of my life is still one of my favorite times to think back upon. The encounters with God I had at that time just absolutely blew me away! One night I remember lying in bed while an actual wind from the Lord blew upon me with force. No windows were open, no powerful fans on, but a steady, rushing wind blew on me and I felt God's tremendous, powerful love and calling. As the wind blew, my feet literally started to burn as if I was on fire. I heard again God speak to my heart He had called me to be a missionary to the nations.

Jesus Himself wants to be the very thing that sustains and strengthens us. When we are not full of the Holy Spirit or abiding in His presence, we can easily run to our old "junk food" to try to fill up for satisfaction. "Junk food" might be defined as anything we run to for a temporary sense of satisfaction that doesn't ultimately strengthen us in Christ. Aside from what is sinful or bad we can run to, the apostle Paul even said things could be lawful, but not beneficial (1 Corinthians 10:23). I know this all too well from experience. Our spiritual bread needs to be Jesus. He wants to fully satisfy our hearts with Himself and His precious presence and love. As we set aside other distractions to sit at His beautiful feet in worship, a great exchange begins to happen. His presence begins to fall on us and His Spirit fills us. We are satisfied.

So often we choose to veg out in front of our computers and the television set or on our cell phones. We try to tell ourselves we deserve it because we have worked hard and are tired. However, when we choose to make Christ our first resting place, we are truly refreshed! I am not saying you can never do this, for certainly there is a healthy time and place for recreation and rest. It's when it becomes our main resting placed, then I believe it is wrong. God wants to be the one who fills us each day with rest in our souls along with empowerment and grace for the day. He wants to be our Bread of Life! Our Manna! The children of Israel were a foreshadow of this when God tested their hearts to see if they would obey Him in the gathering of manna day after day, year after year. He wanted them to rely upon Him for bread, provision, energy, life, and daily strength.

Jesus said in the Beatitudes, "Blessed are those who hunger and thirst for righteousness, for they shall be filled" (Matthew 5:6). Oh, this is really, really good news! He will always fill the hungry with Himself. My husband Wade and I have often remarked we would rather have a truly hungry soul to pour into than any other type of person in the world. God can work with hunger!

God has placed eternity in the hearts of men and women (Ecclesiastes 3:11), and yet at times, we misinterpret it. We search and search for something to fill the great longings in our souls or the great emptiness we feel in our marriages and in our careers that we thought at one time would bring fulfillment. So, we get lost in an old, favorite movie that we watch over and over or maybe a romance novel that takes us away for a time from our present reality. We search for a new gadget, outfit, hairstyle, diet, fad... whatever! Only, those things fall short in the end as well. We were created to love God and be loved by Him. We were created to be a bride.

CHAPTER 2

God Can Meet You Right at Home

I remember a time in my life as a young mom when I had recently given birth to my third child, a darling, baby boy named Josiah.

My husband would host a New Year's gathering each year for men from around the country. They gathered to worship and learn from one another, to evangelize, and to press into God in a special way. Each year these men have met, God has broken through in some life-changing and significant ways. Men have been miraculously healed, delivered, set ablaze with a fresh love for God, and developed a desire for greater holiness and a passion for evangelism. Many men have been called into ministry over the years, and many men have been saved.

One of the yearly highlights of the three-day weekend was testimony time usually taking place after hitting the streets for evangelism. The atmosphere of heaven and expectation usually permeated the air as men shared about the salvations and healings they had witnessed the Father perform by His Spirit in Jesus's Name.

I had three small children, and I had never been able to take part in this time of the weekend because my children were too small to be up so late at night. I had secured my mother-in-law this year to babysit the grandkids. I was beyond hungry for God to touch and speak to me in a life changing way. I had been looking forward to that time with the men for a long time. As the evening wore on and the intensity of the Holy Spirit's presence in the room increased, exciting testimonies poured forth and my dear mother-in-law decided to change her mind. She let me know she preferred to stay in the meeting. I remember my heart sinking and a crushing feeling settling over my emotions. I was so incredibly hungry for God and desperately wanted to receive a touch from heaven. Now, I would be going home with my three, little people to put them to bed alone.

Self-pity filled my heart as I entered my home that night and thought of all God was doing. Once again, I thought, I am left out. I am left behind to care for the kids. I'm pretty sure I was close to tears when I heard the voice of God speak to me very directly. "Katie? Why are you feeling sorry for yourself? I am right here!" Whoa.

I fell on my face in a room we had designated as our prayer room. I told the Lord, "I am so hungry for you, Lord! I want to stay up all night with you just to be with you! I want to be changed! I have got to have you. I've got to have more!" I remember feeling if God didn't touch me, my heart would not be able to take it. My hunger for Him was desperate! I prayed for over an hour or more with no apparent break through when it turned out all my promises and good intentions weren't stronger than my fatigue level. I had been cooking, shopping, meal planning and cleaning up after my family and thirty plus men for three days straight not to mention nursing an infant. I was simply exhausted. I told the Lord how sorry I was for being overcome with fatigue and asked for a bit of sleep. Then I asked Him to wake me up so I could be with Him some more.

I went to bed and fell fast asleep. Sometime in the middle of the night I was awakened with a start. The presence of the Most-High God was in the room. It was absolutely amazing. The power of God began to fall on me. It was incredibly difficult to describe it perfectly, but it felt like wave after wave after wave of electric love pouring through my body. I was completely overcome and overwhelmed with His perfect, holy, powerful love. I remember lying there on my bed that night just curled up in the fetal position with tears streaming down my face while wetting my pillow as the power of God continued to manifest upon me.

Outside that night was a New Year's Eve lightning storm with a thunder and light show I will never forget. I felt it was just for me as I was lying there under the glory feeling His tremendously holy and powerful love crashing in on me. At the same time, I was hearing a song. To this day, I am not sure if it was an audible voice or not. I only know I heard it, and God singing over me, "How He loves" by John Mark McMillan.

He is jealous for me
Loves like a hurricane, I am a tree
Bending beneath the weight
Of His wind and mercy
When all of a sudden
I am unaware of these afflictions

Eclipsed by glory
And I realize just how beautiful
You are and how great your affections
Are for me

Oh, how He loves us so
Oh, how He loves us
How He loves us so

Yeah, He loves us
Woah, how He loves us
Woah, how He loves us
Woah, how He loves

Over and over I heard these words sung and was changed by His awesome love! This was not the first time I had encountered God in such a significant way, but it was one of the most special to me. God taught me that night He responds to hunger! He also taught me He meets wives and mothers right where they are… right in the middle of babies and diapers and fatigue and loneliness! He doesn't need a big, prayer meeting or special conference to break in although He will often use them. He is very happy to meet us right where we are at—home with our children. In fact, He loves to meet us there! Wade and I have been involved with intense ministry for twenty years and through most of that time, Wade has traveled a great deal while I have stayed behind with the children…and God!

Even until this day, I was taken right back to that life-changing moment when I heard that song and for a very long time, I couldn't sing it without crying. I just did not deserve such love, and yet, He lavished it upon me. I was so hungry! Hunger for God is one of the most important things to pray for. It is such a gift. I want to encourage you- His love for you is just as intense. May your hunger be even more intense than mine, and may you be continually filled with awe as you behold His glory! Don't wait. Determine in your heart today to seek Him with all your heart and His promises will truly be realized! "And you will seek Me and find Me, when you search for Me with all your heart" (Jeremiah 29:13, emphasis mine).

CHAPTER 3

Master – My First Love

I can't remember the first person who shared the concept of "Master, Mission, Mate" with me, but it was someone in my college years. The Holy Spirit used it to sharpen my focus and challenge the impact of culture and upbringing in my own life. The basic premise was this: Get to know your Master well. Love Him and cultivate an intimate, dynamic relationship with Him. Focus on Him. Your Master would then allow you the joy of participating with Him in a Mission of some sort. You would receive and sense a confirmation of His calling (for me, this was evangelism at the University of Cincinnati and then onto the mission field of East Africa through Youth With A Mission or "YWAM"). Then for most people while they were loving their Master, following His Mission, one day they would look, and right beside them would be their mates. The lapse of time in-between steps was different for everyone, but I believed wholeheartedly in the "Master, Mission, Mate" mentality. I believed if more parents raised their children to have this mentality the divorce rate would plummet, and the satisfaction level in marriages would be literally supernatural.

As I shared before, a loving and wonderful mother encouraged me to date boys at a very young age. I remember having a conversation with her in high school when she was exhorting me to date as many boys as possible and to have as much fun in my young years as I could. Then, one day I would settle down into a respectful married life and that was that! After the marriage vows were said before God, it would be one man forever until death. "Divorce," she said, "is not to be in your vocabulary."

I respected my mom a great deal for the way she had honored her marriage vows for over fifty years-in good times and bad, in sickness and in heath, in riches and poverty. She truly was an incredible lady! When my father lost his eyesight at the peak of his career, she became his eyes. She carried him through depression, diabetes, and frustration over the losses he endured. I was forever grateful and indebted to her for so many things including the rare ability to look on the bright side of things through trials that would crush most women. I thanked God for her example!

All that said, her advice on dating, though well meaning, was not Spirit-led.

After my laundry room surrender, I began to look at my Master Jesus as my Husband. I began to cultivate an almost romantic relationship with my heavenly Bridegroom, and I have never been the same.

Over the years, I ran across many, many women in ministry who were riddled with self-loathing, feelings of insecurity, abandonment, and rejection. Many looked at themselves through the lens of the world and found there was no hope at all forever attaining the world's standards. Thoughts of, "If only I was more…" (Fill in the blank: beautiful, skinny, smart, industrious, lovable, captivating, gifted, etc.) plagued them day and night. I know; I used to feel the same way. I know what it felt like to look into the mirror and hate the image staring back at me. To even hear the enemy speaking lies into my mind about how ugly, worthless, or inferior I was.

The greatest battle as a woman you will ever face happens right in between your two ears! The mind can be poisoned through a steady diet of American media, failed relationships, father issues, conditional love received as a child, and the list goes on and on. Only by gazing into the eyes of Jesus, filling our hearts and minds with the powerful Living Word, and immersing ourselves in the love of God can we be changed. My exhortation to every single woman who is single was always the same: fall deeply and madly in love with your Master, Jesus. You were ultimately married first and foremost to Him. He is the one who is the perfect Lover of your soul and the ultimate keeper of your heart! In fact, on an almost daily basis for over twenty years now, I have been telling Him that very thing and thanking Him for it!

In practice, what did getting to know your Master look like? Well, for me it looked different at different seasons of my soul, but two things were constant...serious Bible study along with hours and hours of worship and adoration in the secret place on a consistent basis. Many people in the Body of Christ wanted the easy way out for instant arrival at anointing, God-encounters, and maturity. But time revealed over and over God loved me too much to promote me without first pruning me! There are no short cuts to spiritual maturity! Time spent literally meditating on His Word, asking the Holy Spirit to teach me, and putting to death the lies I believed along with false ideas I clung to changed me into His image and brought lasting fruit. I was definitely not the same girl Wade married twenty years ago. Praise God! Yet, I knew I still had so far to go. He never gives up on a hungry heart. "Pursue [literally meaning to aggressively chase like a hunter pursues its prize] holiness," the Bible says, "without which no one will see the Lord" (Hebrews 12:14, clarification mine). There was a definite connection between purity and seeing God. The greater seriousness you had for guarding your heart and not tolerating sin, the more you would see and experience God. "Blessed are the pure in heart, for they shall see God" (Matt 5:8).

As I had gotten to know my Master, I found Him to be beautiful beyond my ability to express, more powerful than I ever imagined in my wildest dreams, more intimately acquainted with the details of my life than previously thought, and altogether good and lovely. His persistent, patient love for me had completely wrecked my heart over and over again. As Misty Edwards sang, "What am I supposed to do with a God so humble? It's breaking me!" I could quite literally speak for days on end about the goodness of my Master. I knew Him, He knew me. I trusted His leadership in any and every situation for He had always proven Himself to be faithful, even when at times I had been unfaithful! Quite simply, I loved Him! And the love I had when I was young and single, though small and weak, He accepted. So, it has blossomed and grown into a more mature love, though no less impassioned. In fact, even more so now, for I love Him so much more!

Your Master knows you intimately. He knows your strengths and weaknesses. He knows every single, last thing about you, including the number of hairs on your head! Psalm 139:1-6 (emphasis mine) said,

O, Lord, You have searched me and known me.
You know my sitting down and my rising up;

24

You understand my thoughts afar off.
You comprehend my path and my lying down,
And are acquainted with all my ways.
For there is not a word on my tongue,
But behold, O Lord, You know it altogether.
You have hedged me behind and before,
And laid Your hand upon me.
Such knowledge is too wonderful for me;
It is high, I cannot attain it.

What a Master we have the privilege and honor to serve! In His intimate, detailed knowing about us, He knows the mission we were best suited for.

One look at young Katie Harrington (my maiden name) and no one, and I do mean no one, would have ever thought, "Oh wow! She's just born for Africa! She looks perfect for marrying the 'Rambo' missionary type!" But, apparently, when my Master looked at me and saw the willingness in my heart, He decided my mission would be among the poorest of the poor on the face of this earth. I was so incredibly grateful.

My calling came after I had cemented Jesus as not only my Lord and Husband but as my Master deep in my heart. I obeyed Him in love even though at times it was weak and frail. I also obeyed Him many times in fear of failing Him. I failed Him many times, but Jesus in His great love and mercy would hear my repentance, wash me, pick me up, and help me into victory again. Slowly, He was changing me. During my sophomore year in college, I began to feel a strong call to go on a mission with God. That wasn't the first time though…

CHAPTER 4

Mission – My Calling

As a second grader growing up Roman Catholic at St. Charles Elementary School in Dayton, Ohio, I remember the day Jesus called me to be a missionary. I had not yet made Him my Savior nor know Him as Master, but in my case, He called me early. That day my teacher Mrs. Holmes assembled the class for a wonderful treat. All the second graders lined up and we walked single file down stairways and through the halls in our little, blue-plaid uniforms to attend a special talk being given by a recent Peace Core volunteer to Africa. We all sat in the cafeteria mesmerized as he showed us his old-fashioned slide show of the places and people he had seen and helped during his year abroad. I was completely drawn in and would later that night write in my diary, "Jesus, when I get older, all I want to do when I grow up is go to Africa and tell people about You." I really believed He heard me. The seed was planted for Him to water when the time became right.

I went to the University of Cincinnati and studied teaching for two years, but in my heart I knew I did not want to be a teacher in America. As my love for Jesus deepened and grew, I was feeding myself with books like No Compromise by Melody Green who wrote about the life of Keith Green. I surrounded myself with people from the Cincinnati Vineyard, which happened to be experiencing renewal at that time. These things solidified a deep sense of calling from God for me to be a missionary. In fact, since the day I came to know Jesus at thirteen, the thought never occurred to me I would ever do anything *but* be a missionary. It was the next logical step... Give your heart to Jesus, then give your life to Jesus.

My former idea of a perfect day would have been: wake up, eat, have time with God, and then hit the streets of Cincinnati for some "servant evangelism." My pastor at that time, Steve Sjogren, had coined the phrase which became the mantra of our church, "love people to Jesus, no strings attached!" I was caught up in the movement. I would get rolls of quarters and head to Sudsy Malone's, a laundry mat/bar for college kids. I plugged people's washing machines with money and told them about the Lord. I plugged expired parking meters with money and left a note on the windshield of the cars explaining what I did and why-because "God loves you, no strings attached!" I left the church address and invited people to services. I can even remember purchasing cigarettes for some squatters in downtown Cincinnati and hanging out with them for the day just telling them about Jesus, reading the Word to them, and loving on them. The cigarettes I figured were a door God was using for me to get to their hearts. I probably wouldn't do that now, but back then I was so young, naïve, and impassioned for evangelism! It was truly awesome. Our church at that time was named one of the fastest growing churches in America due to the mass number of people hitting the streets every day of the week doing random acts of kindness and telling people about Jesus. Many nights of the week, I would gather with other young people just worship God and get into His awesome presence.

So, when our church began to have a number of young people go on the mission field with YWAM (Youth With A Mission), I wanted to be one of them. My parents were pretty worried to say the least. They were certain I had fallen off the deep end. They wanted me to have the kind of "normal" life they had groomed me for: get married to a wealthy man, have kids, and be a housewife who was also a member of the Junior League and the Young Republican's Club. Weekends would be spent cheering on the Fighting Irish of Notre Dame. Above all else, they desired for me to remain Catholic.

In their wrestling with my desires to go on mission with God, they went to seek the counsel of their local priest. He gave them extremely wise advice of which I am certain was Holy Spirit inspired. "Don't give her any of your money to go to YWAM. If God wants her to go, HE will provide for it." Amen!

So, they told me they would not in any way support me to go to the mission field, and they told me I was absolutely forbidden from asking any of their friends for money. I went to prayer and sought the counsel of my Navigator leader at the time. He told me to make a list of the fifty most influential people in my life who were in no way connected with Mom or Dad. Then write to them explaining my desire to join YWAM and ask them to prayerfully and financially support me. I did just that, and it was incredible! I literally had all the money I needed in a very short time.

I chose to go to YWAM Salem in Oregon because the outreaches generally went to East Africa. It proved to be God, and one of the best decisions I have ever made in my life!

For those of you who do not know, Youth With A Mission's first phase for anyone was a Discipleship Training School. It consisted of approximately four months in the classroom and two months of outreach usually overseas. During my first twelve weeks, I grew in so many ways, including but not limited to: servant hood (I was one of three housekeepers for the base), understanding the Father heart of God, spiritual warfare, building biblical relationships, and hearing the voice of God. Those were some of the best days of my young life!

The first day of class will be forever etched in my memory. Our Discipleship Training School, or DTS, was made up of around thirty young adults from all across America and the world. For an ice-breaker, our leader asked each of us one-by-one to get up in front of the class to tell a little about ourselves. Thirty people talking about themselves could get a little long. As the day wore on, I remembered getting a bit fatigued until near the end when one extremely tall, well built, dark haired, and handsome young man got up to speak.

"My name is Wade McHargue," he said. After sharing different things about himself he added, "I just want you to know I have the three of the most beautiful women in the world in my life: my mother and my two sisters, Lauren and Ashley. I am perfectly content with them and with the Lord. In fact, I believe He is calling me to be celibate."

When Wade spoke to the thirty of us, I was all the way in the back of the room and suddenly jolted out of my drowsy state when I experienced supernaturally what felt like a sword piercing my heart. A literal sharp pain shot through me, and I started to feel very agitated in my heart and spirit. At that moment, I turned to the woman sitting next to me and said, "Dana, I need to get some fresh air. What he just said was not God. I need to pray."

I excused myself and went outside to talk to the Lord. "Lord," I said, "I don't feel right in my spirit about what he just said. I mean it sounded so spiritual, but I don't think it was You." I heard the Lord say to me, "You are right, and I want you to pray for him every day, Katie. One hour."

That command was so strongly impressed upon my heart; I had absolutely no precedent for it. I had never prayed one hour a day for anyone before, ever, including myself! I was trying to be a woman of prayer, but it hadn't occurred to me to ever specifically intercede on an every day basis for anyone before. But, I had definitely heard the voice of God. I gave it my best shot. For the duration of our discipleship phase, I was praying every day for Wade. Because I was a housekeeper for three hours each afternoon around the base, I committed my first hour to praying for Wade. During that time, I really began to get God's heart for him, to gain a respect for him, and to get insights into his life from heaven. Every once in a while, the Lord allowed me to share a scripture, an impression, or word with Wade. At those times, Wade said he felt like I was reading his mail so to speak. He said to the Lord, "Lord, why are you revealing these things to her?"

I was not certain how many weeks into school it was when I received a phone call from my mentor, Heather, back in Cincinnati, Ohio, but it wasn't very long. "Katie!" she said, "I ran into Evan Griffin on campus today. He wanted me to tell you he had a dream about you last night. In it you were flying a kite on hill with a really, really, tall guy with black hair."

"Wow, that was crazy because at my school there is this really tall guy here (Wade is 6 foot 8 inches) with jet black hair. But there were no hills and I've never flown a kite with him, so I don't know what it could mean," I responded.

What I didn't realize was it was truly God who had spoken in that dream to Evan Griffin, a man of God. I highly respected Evan who had been my Navigator Bible study leader in college. For him to run into my mentor on campus the very next day and relay the dream for her to share with me was no coincidence. The University of Cincinnati was huge, and they were both busy people who loved me.

About two weeks after the dream incident, we were very blessed to have a missionary/teacher from China arrive to pour into us for one week. Gary Stephens and his wife Helen founded a ministry in Hong Kong named, "Mother's Choice." They focused on rescuing the babies thrown out or abandoned on the streets of China each day due to the One Child Policy.

Gary held evening classes for our DTS, and I remembered clearly the night our class was lined up outside the double doors of the classroom waiting to come in. Gary opened the doors and two-by-two my classmates streamed in and took their seats. I just happened to be standing next to Wade in the double line. When the two of us tried to walk past Gary through the doorway, he literally put both of his hands out to stop us from proceeding. He then looked at us from one to the other and then with wisdom he said, "I want to pray a blessing over you two." He paused, stretched out his hands up high over us and said, "May the LORD bless you and keep you! May He make His face to shine upon you and be gracious to you! The LORD lift up His countenance upon you and give you His peace. In Jesus's name."

Wow! I thought that was bizarre and cool in a really weird way. What did it mean?

A few days later as I was going to my housekeeping job on the base, I passed Gary sitting with our DTS leader inside a gazebo. He called to me, "Katie! Come here!" I walked over and Gary said to me, "What do you think of Wade?"

"I don't know him very well, but from what I have seen I really respect him." I said.

"That's good!" Gary said, with a big smile.

Fast forward one year later for a moment when our friend Nana went overseas to work at Mother's Choice as a short-term volunteer with Gary. One of the first questions He asked her was about us.

"Are Wade and Kate married yet?" She told him we were not married but engaged to be married. "That's good," he said, "God told me they were going to be married." He wisely had not said a word to us and opted instead to pray a blessing over our lives.

Okay. Now rewind backwards to the YWAM class a few weeks after the Gary incident. My heart was full from all the powerful teaching I had been receiving. In YWAM, there was a heavy emphasis on hearing the voice of God for your life. I knew I was called to be a missionary and had known that for a long time, but where?

I set aside some time to sit before the Lord and surrendered that to Him one day. I told the Lord I would go anywhere He asked me to go for Him, but it would be wonderful if He would tell me specifically. As I prayed, a literal word formed in front of my eyes. With eyes wide open, I received a specific word literally written in the air before me: "SENEGAL."

I knew I had heard from God.

I knew absolutely nothing about the country of Senegal. I don't think I had ever even heard of it before let alone knew where it was. This was in the "pre-Google" days and I had no access to the Internet. So, in my excitement I made an appointment with the YWAM career counselor on our base. She scheduled a dinner meeting with me at her home on the following Friday night at seven p.m.

Friday came and I found myself standing on her doorstep with, who else but, Wade!

"What are you doing here?" he asked, looking a bit perplexed.

"I have an appointment at seven," I said.

"But, I have an appointment at seven!" Wade sounded perturbed. He was not excited about sharing his time with this couple.

When they opened the door, they were all apologies. "We are so sorry," the wife said, "My husband scheduled an appointment with Wade, and I scheduled one with you at the same time. Would you guys mind if we all just talked and met?"

What could we say? So, in we went to sit around the table and talk about our callings.

When they turned to Wade and asked him what he wanted to share he said that week he had been actively waiting before God, surrendering his life, and asking God to lead Him where God wanted him to go as a missionary.

He was in a prayer room at the time. Kneeling before a simple chair and pouring out his heart to God when he heard the Holy Spirit speak to his heart, "Look down." Wade looked down and under the chair he was kneeling before was a piece of paper folded up. When he unfolded the paper, it was a fact sheet on the city of Dakar. He received the impression on his heart and mind this city was where God was calling him. So, he went to the career counselor on the base to make an appointment Friday night to talk about how to get from here to there.

After Wade shared, the couple turned to me and asked me to share what God had been laying on my heart. After I shared about the word I had received from God literally written in the air

"SENEGAL," they burst out laughing and praising God with great joy! I had no clue why....

"That was amazing!" they exclaimed. "Dakar is the capitol of Senegal!!! Maybe you'll be on the same team some day! In fact, our base has committed to pray for God to raise up missionaries from here to go to the Wolof People of Senegal! You are the first individuals to respond in answer to our prayers!!!" They were so excited!

I sat there absolutely amazed. God had called us to the same place the same week independently of one another, and He had divinely set this dinner up through an "accident" so we could figure it out.

Mr. Celibate still didn't know what was coming to him though, and so God had a bit more work to do!

Another month passed and we continued to separately chase after God with all of our hearts. Our leadership team began to pair us up for different outreaches and I found our gifts to be very complimentary. But from Wade's perspective, there was nothing really brewing romantically. He was still very committed to celibacy.

Apparently, God still thought it was not good for man to be alone...at least not this one.

CHAPTER 5

Mate–God Was Our Matchmaker

One rainy, Oregon night after a long day of school and work, I was lying in bed exhausted. I was so glad to finally be all stretched out and ready to sleep. It was after curfew time which was at 11 p.m. Curfew could only be broken in one instance and that was if you wanted to go pray in the chapel.

So, lying there that night and listening to the rain outside, suddenly I distinctly heard the Lord say to me, "Get up! Go to the prayer chapel!"

I laid in bed turning the logistics over in my mind. It was raining. I was tired, in bed, in my PJ's, and the prayer chapel required a hike up the side of a small mountain in the dark. I wasn't feeling very obedient.

My heart began to pound like a hammer beating against my chest. Boom! Boom! Boom! "Disobedient! Disobedient! Disobedient! Go!"

I wrestled for some time, maybe twenty minutes, in the misery of knowing I was being disobedient to God. He was calling me to go to the chapel. I must go.

I threw on some clothes but didn't bother with makeup or hair figuring no one was likely to be there this late anyhow as the time was approaching eleven-thirty p.m. by now. I began my wet hike up to the chapel in the dark, and as I approached the chapel doors I suddenly felt an inclination to go to one of the side prayer rooms instead of the main chapel.

As I opened the door of the first prayer room I came to, lo and behold, kneeling inside praying of all people was Wade!

I apologized for walking in on him, went to shut the door when he said, "No, wait! You're supposed to be here. God told me you were coming."

(What?)

You see, Wade had been in the prayer room praying when all of a sudden he heard the Lord speak to his heart, "I'm sending her to you."

He knew exactly who the "her" was. He had patiently been wondering if he had heard incorrectly from the Lord because it had taken me so long to be obedient!

Talk about awkward! We had never been alone before so this was the first time for a heart to heart talk. Wade asked me the question, "So, I know you're called to Senegal, but like, how are you going to get there. I mean, what's your next step?"

Actually, I had been doing a lot of thinking about this on my own. I told him I was thinking about attending a school of tribal medicine through YWAM among the Aborigines in Australia to better prepare for Africa.

Wade shared he was looking into a school of biblical studies in Montana. After we had both shared, Wade said he felt a dagger pierce his heart, which was a physical stab and pain. He felt so sad we would be going in separate directions. Suddenly, Wade said the scales fell from his eyes and he felt the Lord say, "Wake up son! This is your wife!"

The Bible stated the Holy Spirit would bring all things into remembrance God had spoken to you, and at that moment, I had a vivid memory come back to me. I remembered a time, maybe two years previously, when an elderly intercessor at the King's Vineyard in Cincinnati, Ohio, had prayed over me. He had given me a prophetic word from the Lord about the type of man I would marry, and God would reveal him to me at the right time.

At that moment, the right time came. I knew Wade was to be my husband. I became overwhelmed and started to cry. Isn't that just like a woman, ladies?

Wade asked me, "Why are you crying?"

I went ahead and told him about the prophetic word I had received a couple years back at the Vineyard Church about the type of man I was to marry, and God would tell me who it was when I saw him.

Wade, having just realized God was telling Him I was to be his wife, was still in processing mode. He actually became a bit frustrated I told him my story, and he let me know I shouldn't have. He needed to be the one who lead.

That night in the prayer chapel ended a bit awkwardly with me excusing myself and going back down to my bed in a state of bewilderment. I knew God had spoken. Wade was to be my husband. The problem was, even though I knew it, Wade never let on He knew it too.

For the next couple weeks, not a peep came out of Wade's

mouth towards me. In fact, he seemed to avoid me like the plague. What I did not understand was that he was weighing the enormity of the decision and was concerned about our different backgrounds. He was fasting and praying to make sure he had heard God correctly and was asking for more confirmations.

The confirmations came in time. Through our Discipleship Training School, we had the opportunity to go on a two-and-a-half-month mission trip with twelve other young people to Tanzania, Kenya, and the Island of Zanzibar. In that time, Wade and I had the opportunity to see one another in various types of situations which would be very applicable to life on a full-time mission field in Africa for the future. Wade was concerned my "white-bread world" had made me unable to cope with the pressures and harsh realities of life in a third-world country. He was wrong. He could see I adjusted well to the hardships and was sustained by my love for Jesus. During that time, we were both horribly ill with giardia, robbed of our money, evangelized among Muslims, and had long hours of hard, dirty labor shoveling dirt for days at a time. Did I also mention at one point we had little access to bathing of any kind for nearly a *month*? Yes, indeed, my pretty girl exterior was stripped away and under all that dirt Wade said he found the girl of his dreams. After our outreach in East Africa ended, we came back to the States for graduation and to go our separate ways for a season. I moved in with a former college roommate in Cincinnati, Ohio, and worked for a season while Wade moved to Columbia, Maryland, and did the same. However, just a few months later we were engaged to be married and at that time had our very first kiss. We had a three-month engagement and then moved to Chicago, Illinois, where God had led us after much prayer to be further equipped for world missions at the Moody Bible Institute. Those were very happy years. By the time we finally graduated four years and two children later with lifelong, true friends who are still in our lives today, we were sent off to the mission field in Dakar, Senegal, as church planters among Muslims. God was just so good to give me this man as his helpmate in life. I could go into many more details, but I think that was enough. We are currently celebrating 20 years of marriage and have added one more child to the mix to make it three!

CHAPTER 6

The Family Altar

Being a mother to Abigail, Caleb, and Josiah has been the single greatest joy of my adult life. I have loved it every step of the way. Yes, there have been challenging moments and sleepless nights, but I can truly say they have been such a gift, joy, and good company since the day each was born!

Sometimes women noticed my children's good behavior, love for Jesus, or servant heartedness and asked me, "How did you do it?"

I have partnered with God.

Wade has had an extremely busy ministry schedule for most of the years we have been married with kids. He often was gone long hours from our home and often spent nights away due to ministry. For it to be otherwise was the exception not the rule in our home and yet, despite this, I have seen God's faithfulness hearing my constant cries and pleas to Him for help as a mother. I have also consistently asked God to fill in any "gaps" due to the intensity of Wade's ministry and to Father our children.

This was not to say Wade has not been a good father. Wade has intentionally led our family to Jesus for years whenever he was home and into His presence in worship.

We were strong believers in the concept of "The Family Altar." Those of you who have read my husband's book, The Elijah Generation, can read his chapter on that subject, but I would like to put my two cents in as well.

Many times, I have heard frustrated moms share with me their children just weren't hungry for God and just seem to only have an appetite for the things of the world instead of the things of God. Going to church had become just something they did out of a sense of obligation and not love. It was really hard to motivate the unmotivated teen to get into the presence of God especially when they didn't even have a clue what that even means. For sure, starting your kids when they were born was the best plan of all, but if that has not been your story, do not despair. Don't give up! Keep giving the kids opportunities to grow.

I firmly believed in training the palates of our kids. When a good mother worked to place good, well-made, healthy food on the table each day so the kids grew up wanting good, well-made, and healthy food, (opposed to a steady diet of hot dogs, chips, and ice cream creating a desire for food that was bad for us overall) we can train our children's spiritual appetite as well.

Please hear me when I say this next sentence. It might just be the most important part of this entire book: make it the top priority of your parental responsibility to regularly and intentionally get your children into the presence of God.

Let me rephrase this to emphasis my point again.

Do whatever it takes to enter the presence of the living God as often as you can with your children!

Over the years, we have gone through all the stages of this with our three kids: from the newborn stage, to the toddler stage, and up through the teenage years. It just kept getting better and better! In the next chapter, I will cover some practical ways my husband and I have brought our children into the presence of God. I would encourage you to pray and ask the Father if there are things in your home that actually grieve His Spirit and therefore hinder entering His presence. Take these concerns to the Lord and prayerfully present them to your husband in a way which is tactful, humble, and well-thought out. I believe we as wives should keep our spiritual antenna up and not just seeking to keep our houses physically clean, but make sure we are spiritually cleaning them as well.

In our home, we had put a premium on reading and memorizing the Word of God. When the children were small, Wade would tuck them into bed at night and go over memory verses with them until they were memorized.

As soon as they could sing, I would play the "Harrow Family Singers" for them. I highly recommended this for families with children. The Harrow Singers set Scripture to music word for word with the chapter and verse mentioned as well. We had effortlessly memorized a large amount of Scripture at a time with long term memory retention just by playing this music in our home…and the music itself was fabulous too!

Now that our schedules are different, before school each morning and before our family exits the house, Wade or I review Scripture with the kids and often sang a song of praise before sending them out the door. Having committed the day to the Lord with a blessing prayed over them for school, relationships, sports, witness, and specific requests. We prayed together almost every single day as a family! It was a rare day this did not happen at least once. We placed a very high value on the Word of God and prayer. This was where a great deal of good Christian parents stop.

The game changer, in my humble opinion, was when a family delighted in gathering together to worship God with all their hearts.

Since the first day of our marriage, Wade and I have enjoyed extended time in worship together. Most of the time with music and singing, but sometimes we just laid prostrate in quiet adoration or awe.

We never stopped our worship together even when the kids came. We have danced our hearts out until exhausted, sweaty, and tired with worship music cranked up loud with the kids many a time. We have had quiet times of adoration and journaling together as well. In those times together, the Lord had done something far more beautiful than we could have ever hoped for: our kids have fallen in love with Jesus. Through every season of the soul, we as a family have chosen to worship.

I cannot over state the value of just being with God together as a family. Let me illustrate with a simple testimony. We have three kids who were all unique and each responded differently to God. The first two kids loved singing their hearts out to God and seemed to quickly respond to the presence of God. My third child, Josiah, was a very intellectual, analytical kid who did not really enjoy singing (but did love to be with us when we are singing). I had not even seen him fully engage with the Holy Spirit, although like I said, worship, prayer, the Word, etc. were all a daily part of our lives. One night when Josiah was around seven years old, we were having our family worship night. We had lit candles around the living room and turned off the lights. We were cranking up some worship music and the kids and I were dancing before the Lord together. Josiah was quietly off in a corner of the room by himself. Suddenly, the manifest, tangible presence of God came upon my son in a weight of glory. He began to weep with all his heart. He felt the weight of God's glory and love in a life-changing way that night. He has never been the same. He was not an emotional kid by nature, but when God's presence came upon him, he entered the heart of God. I remembered another day this happening during home school. We often prayed through Operation World for unreached people groups to come to know Jesus. One day as we were praying, Josiah again came under the strong spirit of intercession and he began to weep, groan, and cry out in prayer with such force and unction for a young boy. He stayed totally connected to God in earnest prayer for 45 minutes straight. He was crying out with all his heart for the world to know Jesus. These encounters with God have happened to each of my kids and in the context of family worship together. There is a saying, "Once you have experienced God's glory, you are forever ruined for the ordinary." This has been our heart cry as parents to get our children into the glory of God.

Often, I tell moms who were frustrated about the *how* of family worship through a simple example of how to get started.

If you were unaccustomed to getting into the presence of God with your children and spouse, then I think a really great place to start was with a "family council."

As parents, call the family together for a time of repentance starting with you. Let your children know you have blown it by not putting a premium upon worshipping God together as a family. Tell them God was revealing to you how much you needed Him and how sweet it was to worship together as a family. Repent in humility before the kids. I think most kids, upon seeing the earnest and heartfelt humility of mom and dad, will be drawn in by that alone.

Next, for those of you with kids who were unaccustomed to times of extended worship, I believed in setting an atmosphere in your home that sent a clear message to everyone this time was special and different.

For me, this had often meant tidying up the living room, lighting candles all around, and shutting off any exterior lights or competing noise. I would then load up my I-Pod with worship music, sometimes dance music and other times more contemplative, and we would simply play it and enter in. You take the lead as a parent. Kids will begin to feel more comfortable as they see their parents engaging with God through all their hearts and bodies! You may do this once a week in the beginning. It may start out with a couple of songs, but over time I would encourage you to let the kids know ahead of time everyone is going to worship, pray, and listen for a set time. It could be 10 minutes at first, but as the family grows and the worship time becomes expected, the time can eventually be an hour or longer. You should gauge this so it's truly a desire, not something just forced.

I have seen other people who literally have enough room in their homes to create a room set aside exclusively for prayer and worship. It is decorated accordingly…simple pillows thrown around the floor, inspirational artwork on the walls, maps of the world marked with missionaries and ministries, the Bible accessible, and candles or even incense lit sending forth beautiful fragrance. (Obviously, we cannot all do this, so if you just have a simple living room, like us, it's okay)

Some kids who have never "worshipped" God before outside of a church building (that's part of the problem, we are the church, and we don't need to go to a building to have a worship service) might feel awkward at first. That's okay. Keep encouraging them to press into God. Often, I would read a passage of Scripture describing God found in Revelation 4 and 5 right before or during worship. Then I encouraged my children to close their eyes and envision it as if they were there before the throne of God themselves just laying it all down before Him.

Over the years, our kids had begun to read aloud the scriptures on their own and bless the whole family with what God was speaking to them. Many times during family worship nights, we ended up praying over our kids, blessing them, and ministering to them right where they were.

Another practice our family had done for years was taking communion together. We broke up some matzo crackers and got a cup of grape juice. Then Wade or I read a passage of scripture like Matthew 26:26-29, and we encouraged our kids to confess their sins to God or to one another if they needed restoration in a family relationship. We often did this right before worship time so we knew we were entering into God's presence with clean hearts, and we weren't weighed down by sin and shame. This has been such a healing time over the years.

Bottom line: Make worship together as a family a priority! It's never too late to start! Let it start with you! Setting the atmosphere of your worship space can actually be a simple tool that shifts your children's hearts to worship. If this seems awkward at first, keep at it!

CHAPTER 7

Kids Who Know God, Love the World but Aren't of the World

It may be said perhaps there are four different types of kids in the world:

1) Those who are passionately loving and living for Jesus who have an offensive posture with appropriate engagement in the world for the advancement of His Kingdom

2) Those who don't know Jesus at all and are completely lost

3) Those who love God and are striving to live lives of holiness but have decided engaging with the world is too scary and might contaminate them

51

4) Those who have grown up in the church and call themselves Christians but talk like the world, act like the world, dress like the world, watch the movies of this world, play the games of this world, and hold to the standards of this world.

If any of the last three groups are your kids, it's time to do some serious repentance as a mom. We cannot control our husbands and how they lead our family, but we can humble ourselves before God and our children. Now is the time to make a serious stand in our homes and on behalf of our kids. From here on out, as far as it concerns you, you will not be the one feeding your kids the world.

Your home as a mother is your sphere of influence like no other place in the world. Your children are your first disciples, and you can carry them before the throne of grace to God in a way no one else can do. If my children were walking in compromise or did not have God's heart for the world, I would be proactively pleading with God to intervene in their lives and giving my home to Him in prayer. I would be making it my practice to bless each room and life represented by the room as I clean. I would be getting on my face before God with fasting and crying out to the Living God to move in their hearts bringing hunger and thirst for righteousness to them.

One word of caution: If you are married to a man who is not walking in personal holiness, you are still called by God to reverence him. This can be difficult, but not impossible. Get on your face in prayer and ask God to fill you with His love and respect for your husband. You have been called by God to be your husband's helpmate and not his personal Holy Spirit spokesperson.

The Word of God says,

*Wives, likewise, be submissive to your own husbands,
that even if some do not obey the word, they, without a
word, may be won by the conduct of their wives, when
they observe your chaste conduct accompanied by
fear. Do not let your adornment be merely outward—
arranging the hair, wearing gold, or putting on fine
apparel—rather let it be the hidden person of the
heart, with the incorruptible beauty of a gentle and
quiet spirit, which is very precious in the sight of
God. For in this manner, in former times, the holy
women who trusted in God also adorned themselves,
being submissive to their own husbands, as Sarah
obeyed Abraham, calling him lord, whose daughters
you are if you do good and are not afraid with any
terror.* (1 Peter 3:1-6, emphasis mine)

I have watched marriages destroyed by well-meaning
women who in frustration would time and again put their foot down
assertively and try being the voice of God to their man. Rarely did
that work well. God's plan of respect was best. God really is able to
get through to thickheaded men.

Maybe you have seen the kind of kids I have described in
the first group. They are a Jesus generation who are the hope of
tomorrow. They are unashamed of God, worshippers who trust God
and rely upon the Holy Spirit in dependence each day. They are not
perfect, but their hearts are set on loving obedience to the One they
love and know. This kind of kid is your goal.

They have been raised on a steady diet of the Word, prayer,
worship, and selfless service to others. It is never too late start.

One event Wade and I deem as incredibly important in the

lives of our children was their thirteenth birthday. At that time, we had a 'rite of passage' for each of them, which included the biggest birthday party of their lives and some sort of weekend away with one of us. For our first daughter Abigail, her Grandma Linda and I took her away for a weekend to Gettysburg, Pennsylvania. We stayed at a lovely Victorian bed and breakfast for the weekend spending time doing things girls love to do...checking out antiques, shopping, eating out, etc. But the most important time was when Grandma Linda and I spent time with Abigail pouring into her heart as a young woman. We spent an intensive time teaching her the facts of life, as well as what being a true lady looks like and following God with all her heart. Emphasizing God's plan of waiting for marriage before having sex was the best design of all. After our fun weekend away, we arrived home to a huge party tent set up by our guys where we had a party with everybody, and Abigail received a beautiful purity ring from her dad. Then Wade took Abigail out on a date, and they had a great time. Abigail loves roller coasters so they had a blast laughing and screaming at Hershey Park. It was a highlight of her life, and a capstone on her early training.

When our son Caleb turned thirteen, we celebrated a rite of passage for him as well. Wade had Caleb plan a trip to climb the tallest mountain in the Continental United States, Mt. Elbert in Colorado. Wade did not help him with the planning of this trip. He was trying to teach Caleb preparedness, thinking through what was necessary to bring or not bring, and teaching Caleb leadership skills. Caleb understood if he failed to be prepared with correct directions (all the way from South Dakota to Colorado and back), or failed in preparing all the supplies they both needed, they both would suffer. Caleb and Wade both successfully summited Mt. Elbert! Caleb did an outstanding job leading the trip and during that grueling climb learned about being a man. Here are some of the observations and lessons he learned on his rite of passage:

What I learned on My Climb to the Top of Mt. Elbert

Caleb McHargue

1. Be responsible; make wise choices on what to bring and find out where to go. If I don't bring it, it's my fault. I also need to be responsible for those I lead to make sure they are equipped for the journey.
2. Push yourself. While climbing, I was learning I have to push myself physically and mentally.
3. Life is like a mountain. During life, you will face challenges (like the wind, sun, and steepness) …overcome them with determination.
4. Vision! You need to have a goal; a summit to reach for. I need vision in my life.
5. Be prepared to set little goals. I learned how setting smaller goals helps you get to the bigger goal. It made it more attainable.
6. Walk by faith and not by sight. By sight, it can be discouraging like when we came to two false summits.
7. Enjoy the journey. Don't get so focused on the summit I miss the beauty around me.
8. We need to have time to rest or you can hurt yourself and start to be careless.
9. Be a leader which means to be an encourager, have a clear vision, be prepared, have determination, make wise choices, be more concerned for people than for the goal,

be able to adjust, and be flexible.

10. Sometimes the higher we go, the harder it gets (like with spiritual warfare).

11. Don't be discouraged if the higher you go the fewer people may come with you (not everyone who started ended up finishing).

12. People who are sacrificial for the same goal are in unity (like the other mountain climbers were encouraging to each other).

13. Be careful where you step, because it could affect people behind you (when we were climbing on shaky rocks, being careful to have a sure foot so we didn't fall on someone below).

14. Be careful of the contagious disease of complaining. It can spread fast!

15. Rely on God; ask Him for strength in the journey. (Philippians 4:13)

I hope these rite of passage ideas encouraged your family to do something similar! These two memories with our kids were so special and were such a time of bonding and blessing. When Caleb and Wade reached the summit of Mt. Elbert, Wade prayed a fathers' blessing upon him and spoke over his life words of affirmation and destiny just as I did with my daughter Abigail during our time together. When raising kids who lived in the world but weren't of the world, I really believed giving them an alternative that was so much richer, so much more satisfying and meaningful ensured their hearts wouldn't go astray when temptation called.

CHAPTER 8

Spiritual Warfare in Marriage and Ministry

Ladies, in my nearly twenty years of marriage, I have experienced my fair share of spiritual warfare. One of the easiest ways for the enemy of our souls to attack is in our marriages. I don't know about you, but in speaking for myself, when Wade and I got married, even though we had such a clear and obvious calling to one another from God we realized very quickly we were opposites on the personality spectrum. In the beginning, I was an extrovert (loved being with people) and Wade was an introvert (loved being alone). I was intuitive (didn't know why I knew things, I just knew them) and Wade was sensing (if he could see it, touch it, taste it, feel it, then it was a reality). I was a feeler; Wade was a thinker. I was a person who could see easily both sides of every story and find the grey middle. Wade was very black and white and saw things as right or wrong. As you could imagine, this did not make marriage always easy-peasy. I was last born, a free spirit while Wade was first-born, who wanted order, was very driven, saw the goal and would pay the high price to get to it (even pulling me with him if necessary).

When you combine all of our differences with the type of calling God had placed on our lives for being in full-time ministry as missionaries in the Muslim world and all of the pressures that came with living cross culturally (learning new languages—we've learned three outside of English) while raising kids...you've basically got a recipe for the perfect storm outside of the grace of God.

I am telling you, the enemy wants to kill, steal, and destroy you, your marriage, and your children. He will do what he can to find a way to if you let him. I do not want to exalt Satan to any greater position than as a created being under the ultimate authority of God, but I have experienced times of intense spiritual warfare with him in my life.

If you want to be effective against the enemy, you need to know how he fights...and it's dirty, wickedly dirty. This is a war and that is the language of the New Testament (see Philippians 2:25; Philemon 1:2; 1 Timothy 1:18; 2 Timothy 2:3-4, 4:7; 1 Peter 2:11). We as followers of Jesus are engaged in a very real, spiritual war. We are called to overcome and be victorious through our Lord Jesus. We must use the Bible as our handbook for living in this world and to see the marriage our Father God wants for us. To be able to overcome and be victorious, we are also called to be wise. The Scriptures reveal to us how the enemy works and seeks to fight against us.

In 2 Corinthians 2:11, Paul states that Satan is not to take advantage of us "for we are not ignorant of his devices."

What are the devil's schemes or devices? Here is a list of

some of the ways we have seen the devil seek to get a foothold in our own lives and what we have observed in others' marriages and families. I hope as you read through this list you will pray through it as well. Search your heart for anything God might be revealing for you to deal with.

1.) Unforgiveness

When asked, "What is the secret to your successful marriage?" Billy Graham answered, "I can sum it up in one word: Forgiveness."

How can we forgive? We must remember Jesus's words in Matthew 18 and put in context He has forgiven us even though He's never done us wrong. So, we must forgive others.

Jesus was clear: if we do not forgive our husbands (or anyone who has wronged us) we cannot receive forgiveness from God (Mark 11:26). C.S. Lewis said rightly, "To be a Christian means to forgive the inexcusable, because God has forgiven the inexcusable in you."

Forgiveness is not an emotion nor dependent on emotions. It is an act of the will. As Corrie Ten Boom, a survivor of the holocaust, who lost her family and endured unspeakable horrors at the hands of her Nazi persecutors said, "Forgiveness is an act of the will, and the will can function regardless of the temperature of the heart."

The enemy seeks to put a root of bitterness in our hearts, but we must be quick to come before the Lord with a heart check and make sure the seed has no way of being planted to become a root in our hearts. Many times, in my twenty years of marriage I have run to the Lord and gotten on my face before God in a place of hurt from some misunderstanding between Wade and me. When I cried out my heart before God and asked Him to remove all hurt, bitterness, and anger by replacing it with His love for Wade instead—God did it. I simply choose to forgive…whether or not my husband asked for forgiveness. The Bible said, "Blessed are the peacemakers, for they shall be called the children of God" (Matthew 5:9). This is not to say we don't deal with problems, but I have found there was a best time for everything. And for us, in the heat of the moment was usually the worst time to talk. After we've both had the opportunity to meet with Jesus, it was much easier to talk through what was upsetting both of us.

2.) Unrighteous anger

In Ephesians 4:26-27, we are commanded to not "give place to the devil, and don't let the sun go down on your anger." Again, this is connected to forgiveness, but it also means to be on guard against frustrations and festering irritations. Thomas Fuller stated something well concerning anger, "Two things a man should never be angry at: what he can help, and what he cannot help." In other words, if there is something we can do to fix the situation, don't get angry, just do what you can do. If it's something you can't do anything about, then it must be surrendered to the Lord! Anger is rooted in control and wanting to control someone or something. When we surrender that which is out of our control to the Lord, we walk in peace. What a blessed peace it is! So, check yourself. Is there something you need to place in God's hands? He cares for you, so don't keep it and let it eat you up.

3.) Bringing up the past

There is not a single person alive on the face of the earth today over the age of three who has not engaged in some sort of sinful or hurtful behavior at one time or another. We have all needed forgiveness. So let's be quick to not dwell upon the faults of others. The word "devil" means slanderer or accuser, so when we are bringing up past hurts and accusing others, we are participating in the devil's work. We are partnering with him in what his very nature is. This would be a good reminder to all. I would suggest you go to your husband in a time of peace and unity. Give a commitment to each other you won't participate in the enemy's work in this way. Recognize when the devil is trying to bring bad memories into your mind to take your thoughts captive and reject them in Jesus's name!

4.) Worldliness

We know the devil is called "the god of this world" (2 Corinthians 4:4). We must be on guard against allowing the world into our hearts and minds. The Bible is clear in James 4:4, "friendship with the world is enmity with God," and 1 John 2:15 is clear, "if anyone loves the world, the love of the Father is not in him." Be on guard against backsliding, letting your guard down, and excusing things that are watched or listened to which grieve the Holy Spirit. Proverbs 14:14 states, "The backslider in heart will be filled with his own ways." When there are media, books, or video games that glorify violence, horror, pornography, anger, vulgarity, alcoholism or drug abuse, marital infidelity, promiscuity, gambling, materialism, outward appearance, fame, and fortune as the high goals....it is to be rejected and abhorred. For some of you, it might be time to check your movie collection or cancel your cable bill.

5.) Pride

We read in 1 Chronicles 21, Satan put it in David's heart to "count" his greatness and accomplishment doing so brought upon him God's judgment. Paul warns in 1 Corinthians 10:12, "Therefore let him who thinks he stands take heed lest he fall." We must be on guard against putting trust in our own abilities, experiences, or knowledge and be sure to give God glory for everything good in our lives. We all need God's grace, and He said He only gives grace to the humble.

6.) Quarreling spirit

A quarreling spirit is many times connected to pride: we believe we are right, we know what is best, and only we have a handle on the truth. The Bible says in Proverbs before contention is pride. In 2 Timothy 2, we read one who is always arguing and quarreling can in fact become captives to the enemy, and they will do what Satan wants them to do. Guard against that strife, and make sure in your home you will hold James 1:19 high as the standard, to "be swift hear, slow to speak,slow to wrath."

7.) Believing lies about ourselves or about others

This is big. We see Jesus calls the devil "the father of lies" in John 8:44. It is Satan's strategy to get us to believe lies about ourselves or about others. These lies, if they continue to be believed in, become strongholds. These can include thoughts of you "needing" something for comfort (addictions). Constantly being cynical can be evidence of someone believing things the enemy wants them to focus on instead of God's Word which says, that love "bears all things, believes all things, hopes all things, endures all things," in 1 Corinthians 13:7. Strongholds can come through declarations over oneself or others such as "I can never change…" or "this is just how I am" … or accepting compromise during sinful thinking like, "This isn't as bad as what I used to do"…"I at least can have this…" Anything that justifies sin is not of God but is a lie of the evil one.

8.) False vows/ broken promises

According to Matthew 5:37, Jesus reveals the enemy wants to get us to make false vows to lead us in broken promises and lack integrity. Why? Leviticus 5:4 tells us this is a trespass before God, and according to James 5:12, this could lead us into being judged. It's very important to remember: no integrity = no authority. If you don't have integrity in your speech or actions, you will lose the respect of your spouse and your children. Jesus said we'd be held accountable for every idle word. Our family especially should know they can take our word to the bank—what we say we mean, and what we mean we say. Don't make rash vows or even say "I will do that…" and you don't do it. God will hold us to this vow and so will people. Many children have lost respect for their parent(s) because of this issue. You may need to ask forgiveness for broken promises and careless words. Pray like David and ask for a guard over your mouth and be diligent in this (Psalm 141:3).

9.) Fear

We read in 2 Timothy 1:7, "God has not given us a spirit of fear, but of power and love and a sound mind." If your heart is gripped with thoughts of fear, such as fear of your husband leaving or cheating on you, or you fear your kids failing, dying, or getting sick—this is from the enemy. You must reject those thoughts and meditate on God's Word, which feeds our faith (Romans 10:17). Faith and fear can't co-exist anymore than love and fear. We must ask our Father as Paul taught in Ephesians 3 to pray for our growth in His love that even surpasses knowledge. His perfect love will drive out all fear (1 John 4:18). A.B. Simpson said, "Fear is born of Satan. If we would only take time to think a moment, we would see everything Satan says is founded upon a falsehood."

Amy Carmichael said, "If my attitude be one of fear, not faith, about one who has disappointed me; if I say, 'Just what I expected', if a fall occurs, then I know nothing of Calvary love." Our faith is in Jesus and His Word. He has proven His love for you and me by dying on the Cross. He is wholly trustworthy.

Let us remember the weapons of our warfare are mighty through God! They pull down these strongholds, and we have the ability to take every thought captive to make it obedient to Jesus (2 Corinthians 10:3-5). What a joy to be set free and no longer a slave!

The Scriptures tell us we are first to submit to God then resist the devil. You and I cannot resist the devil if we are not submitted to God. How do we know if we are submitted to God? We are walking in peace. If you have emotions of anger, irritability, worry, or fear, it reveals the situation is not submitted to God. Areas we must continually submit to God are: our health, marriage/family (do you feel you are constantly trying to "fix" your spouse or are over protective of the kids?), finances (are they submitted to God or are you in charge?), relationships (is there anger with someone who has done you wrong?), the future (do you worry about the future?), and our reputation (do you have to defend yourself, or get angry if someone is talking about you behind your back?).

Let's remember the battlefield is in the mind, but Jesus has given us victory through:

1. Himself, our Lord Jesus (1 John 3:8; Ephesians 1:20-23)
2. His Mighty Name (Mark 16:17,18)
3. Through His blood (Revelation 12:11)

4. Our testimony (Revelation 12:11)
5. Not loving our lives even to death (no fear! Revelation 12:11)
6. Our faith (in Him and His Word, 1 John 5:4)
7. Praise and worship! (Praise is a weapon that directly come against depression, inward focus, or despair. Look at what the Lord did in response to Paul and Silas' worship (Acts 16)! Through God's army in 2 Chronicles 20, we are told in Psalm 106:47, "we triumph in His praise!")
8. Fasting: (This is a powerful weapon especially to combat unbelief (see context of Matthew 17:20-21). The issue Jesus addressed wasn't the demon or the "size" of it. The problem was the disciples' unbelief, and Jesus said this "kind" of unbelief (see context) comes out by prayer and fasting. Fasting has a way of placing true hunger in our hearts for the Lord and the ability to believe for His breakthrough through faith in His precious promises. I've seen God bring breakthroughs in my own marriage by way of fasting.)
9. And, of course, Jesus has given us the armor of God. (Ephesians 6:10-18) which we see is all rooted in the Word of God (faith, righteousness, preparation of sharing the Gospel, the knowledge of salvation, truth, and the sword of the Spirit).

Remember, no army consists of loners. We need each other to pray for each other. Let's make sure it doesn't turn into a complaining or gossip session, but a sincere heart of love and faith to pray for each other for change so our King will be glorified. Amen?

CHAPTER 9

Capturing Our Kids Hearts and Minds for God

Everyone longs to be important. Everyone longs to have purpose, vision, and a reason to live. We were created by our Creator God to long for these things so in our dissatisfaction we would reach out for Him and find Him. Only in Him can our hearts be fully satisfied. Those who do not know God, and I mean really don't know Him, are spending their energies on causes and projects hoping to find a sense of satisfaction and well-being inside. Adolf Hitler knew this well as he projected the future greatness of His country upon the greatness and energy of Germany's millions of youth. He created a powerful force called "The Hitler Youth."

"Formed officially in 1926, the Hitler Youth offered its members excitement, adventure, and new heroes to worship. It gave them hope, power, and the chance to make their voices heard. And for some, it provided the opportunity to rebel against parents, teachers, clergy, and other authority figures." (Hitler Youth, Growing up in Hitler's shadow, Bartoletti pg. 7) Adolf Hitler admired the natural energy and drive young people possess. He understood young people could be a powerful, political force that could help shape Germany's future. In his quest for power, Hitler harnessed their enthusiasm and loyalty.

"I begin with the young," said Hitler. "We older ones are used up…but my magnificent youngsters! Are there finer ones anywhere in the world? Look at all these men and boys! What material! With them I can make a new world!" (ibid pg. 7)

We are seeing the same thing in our day and age in the Middle East. Muslims are training children to be American and Jew hating killers. They are being indoctrinated at a very young age to hate, kill, and think of suicide bombing as an honorable career choice while striving for Jihad around the world.

It has been said in our nation, "the hand that rocks the cradle rules the world." This is in a very real sense true.

It is time for true, God-fearing, sin-hating, non-compromising mothers to arise!

Our country is in a very real battle right now between light and darkness. I maintain a position I have held for a very long time: one of the greatest hopes we have for America and this world is mothers who are actively making true disciples of their children. Ladies, we will be a powerful force to be reckoned with when we get our acts straight and get serious about submitting ourselves fully to God in our homes and passing that along to our children. May God get all the glory for your life of faithful surrender and active discipleship! Mind you, your primary motivation for everything you do, is love for Jesus, which is, after all the greatest and most powerful weapon.

Training our children to be people who grow up and carry the heart of their King and the wisdom and character to advance the

King's Kingdom, starts with you.

As you start each day, do you start by scrolling through your phone or on your knees? God forgive us! I find the days I have begun intentionally with God at the forefront of my consciousness are the days I walk in greater impact. You cannot give what you do not have yourself. Ladies, you need to train yourself to surrender your day to the Lord. Wake up a little earlier if you need to, but make sure you have a quiet time with Jesus! When my kids were very tiny, it didn't always happen in the morning because if I would wake up, they would wake up. God knows this and understands. Don't be discouraged...He totally gets what moms go through! The important thing is: carve it in! Ideally, when I am fresh in the morning is when I find I am best able to sit quietly (with my coffee!) and read the Word often praying and talking to God at the same time. Right now I have a goal to read at least five chapters a day. Often I read more, but I find this is a good pace to really feel as though I have feasted on God's Word. As I read, I can often feel a palpable sense of the presence of the Holy Spirit. I am tuned into God's thoughts and personality as I read His Word, and if I miss this time, I literally feel distracted and discontent throughout the day. Other times, I have been involved in Bible study groups working in a workbook of some sort. The important thing is: get in the Word, and let the Word get into you! It really does change us, renew our minds, and strengthen our faith. I find myself falling in love with God over and over again.

Do not negate time on your knees or your face before God. It is good to humble yourself physically before God if you are able. Many times as I lay prostrate before God, I have found envisioning Revelation 4 and 5 in my mind helps in my worship and getting the right perspective: God = big; Katie = small! Many times my problems are the things taking over my heart and causing me to lose peace and joy, but as I gaze upon my beautiful God who is seated upon His sapphire throne surrounded by twenty-four elders, cherubim, and seraphim worshipping Him day and night, night and day. Well, my problems just don't seem so big anymore! I realize He is all-powerful, all-knowing, perfect in holiness, wisdom, and He is perfectly able to care for me! This is a great place to begin your day…on your face.

We have an unbelievable promise from God in 2 Corinthians 3:18,

But we all, with unveiled face, beholding as in a mirror the glory of the Lord, are transformed into the same image from glory to glory, just as by the Spirit of the Lord.

Wow! Just wow!

When the apostle Paul wrote this verse under the inspiration of the Holy Spirit, the mirrors he looked into every day to check his hair were a whole lot different than the mirrors we look into today. When I look into a mirror, the image staring back at me, like it or not, is a true and accurate image. I can see every fine line starting to form on my face, every grey hair, and every single dimple on my body. I can see the good things too. When Paul looked into a mirror, it was a different story. The mirrors of ancient Rome were molten bronze which had been highly polished to give a reflection of a face. Paul said in 1 Corinthians 13:12 (AMP),

For now [in this time of imperfection] we see in a mirror dimly [a blurred reflection, a riddle, an

enigma], but then [when the time of perfection comes we will see reality] face to face. Now I know in part [just in fragments], but then I will know fully, just as I have been fully known [by God].

So, essentially in 2 Corinthians 3:18, when Paul spoke of "beholding as in a mirror the glory of the Lord," he was saying even a blurred, dim image of God, if beheld by a child of God, had the ability to transform us into His same image from glory to glory. In other words, gazing upon God and using the passages of Scripture where He communicates with us what He looks like, what He is like, and meditating upon them however dimly transforms us. As we behold Him, we become like Him. So will our children. This is a promise from God.

So often we spend the majority of our time beholding the world in one way or another when what will really make us more Christ like is spending time looking at God. When we become enthralled by God's beauty and majesty, when we behold Him as the great God He is who wraps Himself in light as with a garment and sits enthroned on high who has a rainbow around him as a symbol of His covenant of mercy to the nations, we become undone. We realize the rightness of His judgments on the earth. He and what He chooses to do or not do no longer offends us. We realize He is perfect in beauty, holiness, and wisdom.

I have entered a new season of my life. After 8 years of home schooling, we as a family all felt God calling our children to the public school. It has been a good thing in their lives, and they were ready for it. My youngest son, Josiah was attending a one-room, Christian schoolhouse for two years where I volunteered as the music teacher. Last year, we decided to home school him for one more year. Our private school only went through second grade, and he was a third grader this year. So rather than put him into our public school just yet (which was very good by the way), we decided another year at home with me to pour into him would be beneficial.

This morning Josiah and I started school very early. His dad was taking him away for a day to have some father/son time, so I wanted to get school done first thing. We sat on the couch together. Me with my coffee, and Jo in his PJs as we read the Word of God together first thing. Our passage was taken from Hebrews 4:1-13. The passage was entitled, "The Promised Rest." A passage that spoke of honoring the Sabbath Day. God said in His word,

> *There remains therefore a rest for the people of God. For he who has entered His rest has himself also ceased from his works as God did from His. Let us therefore be diligent to enter that rest, lest anyone fall according to the same example of disobedience.*
> (Hebrews 4:9-11)

I asked Josiah the question, "What efforts can help us enter into God's rest?" We talked about getting quiet before God and intentionally entering into His presence. I then asked him the question, "How would you explain the 'promised rest' to someone who was not a believer in Jesus?" It was so interesting to hear his answer. Remember, he was a third grader. He told me when he would get quiet and focuses on God, he could feel God's presence. Josiah described it like a blanket over his heart that made his heart burn within him. He said when he was in the presence of God, he had peace in his mind and rest.

How beautiful! How aptly spoken by a mere 9-year-old. No wonder God said we are to become like children!

Unfortunately, I have seen too many children and even children of those who are in ministry who have no hunger for the presence of God only great, big appetites for the things of this world. How sad.

Momma, it is your job to whet your children's appetites on a regular basis for the presence of God. Posture your heart to abide with Christ, and then lead your children to posture their hearts to do the very same thing. Turn off the video games, the TV, the Internet, and get on your faces together before God! You will never regret it! Enter into the rest God has promised you, together...and please, don't just wait for Sunday!

CHAPTER 10

Moms, Don't be Ninnies!

Train up a child in the way he should go,
And when he is old he will not depart from it.
(Proverbs 22:6)

He who spares his rod hates his son,
But he who loves him disciplines him promptly.
(Proverbs 13:24)

It is grievous to meet children, even children of Christian parents mind you, who are very unpleasant to be around. Children who whine, complain, backbite, hate their parents, bully and require much coaxing to be helpful or obedient are not being parented biblically. This has brought us to our knees in prayer many, many times. There are many reasons for this: Parents who are constantly too busy with "ministry" to bother with making disciples out of the very children God has given them; a steady diet of the world being brought into the home for consumption in the form of media, internet and video games, books, etc., and parents who just want to be "best buds" with little Johnny or Sally instead of doing the hard work of training and disciplining them!

Ladies, we cannot control the sort of fathers our husbands are to our children, but we can control the way we train and discipline. Above all, please don't be afraid to parent!

There have been a few times I have sought to cook a delicious, healthy meal for guests whose children take one look at it and say, "I don't like that!" (without even trying it). Then the entire family was forced to watch the embarrassed mother coax and squirm while her defiant child refused to budge. I remember one child refusing to eat anything I prepared with the exception of peaches and pizza for three days making everyone embarrassed and uncomfortable at the spectacle he was making was then given on a nightly basis a hearty bowl of ice cream! That child knew sure as the sun would set and rise each day, he could count on his nightly, sweet treat to pull him through! He told me so himself!

I have seen siblings who hate each other, fighting, bickering, and name calling with a stomach sickening consistency. All of these examples are children of nice Christian parents, but nevertheless, parents who have not successfully trained their children to love God, love one another, or prefer one another above themselves. This teaching must come out of our actions and words day and night, week after week, year after year. We need to train our children to obey us instantly. In fact, their lives may just depend upon it! Children know when we mean what we say. I always find it amazing the same children who will not listen to their own moms and dads will often obey me. They know I mean what I say.

When my children were very small, I started to train them. As I wrote earlier, we always began each day worshipping God together. I would read the Bible to them, or we would sing the Word together. Often, we would take nature walks together where we would praise God for all the magnificent creation He had made. We would start and end each day in prayer. We began each meal with thanks to the One who had provided it. Then we spent time praying for others around the world and those in our sphere of influence. We did not try to shelter our kids from the real hurts of real people, but instead, we prayed and ministered to them. Our home was a refuge of love and shelter from the world. I was not a perfect mother, nor am I today, but I can say when I have failed, I have sought to model for them repentance and brokenness. This was all a part of training.

I also trained them from the beginning to obey me without needing to raise my voice. When my babies were small, if they were touching something I did not want them to touch, I would say a firm but calm, "No." I often punctuated this with a small flick of my finger to reinforce my point. They learned very quickly I meant what I said. The small flick didn't hurt them, but it did startle them. You see, if a child was consistently loved and cared for, protected and sheltered, when physical discipline needed to be administered, there was no resentment. They knew nothing but love, and discipline was no different. Discipline was for their protection and well-being. Discipline, administered correctly, is love.

As they grew older, if they would not obey a command I knew they could accomplish such as, "Abigail, go get that book for me." If my child said, "No!" or her body language let me know she understood but did not want to obey, I would calmly look her in the eye and tell her, "Abigail, Mommy just told you to get that book. You did not obey me. God says you need to obey Mommy. I am going to have to spank you one time." (Or three times…depending on age and seriousness of situation. Running into a street without looking was far worse than not bringing a book.) I put her little, diaper-padded bottom over my knees and gave her a spank. Then I put her down on the ground and gave her the firm command again, "Abigail, go get that book." Usually, she would then go get the book. If she did not, I would calmly repeat the exact same thing again. After she bought me the book, I hugged her and told her I loved her. I then sat her on my lap, held her close, and prayed for her to be obedient next time. I thanked Jesus for forgiving her, and giving Abigail the opportunity to say she was sorry to receive forgiveness. Then, we moved on. In this way, I trained her to be obedient to me. I treated each and every disobedience the same way. My children grew up knowing that obedience = blessing; disobedience = discipline.

Let me interject with this:

Before disciplining, I believed it was very important to tell your children exactly what the punishment would be for their disobedience. For example, "Abigail, you did not obey Mommy right away when I told you to clean up your toys. This makes me very sad. If you do not learn to obey Mommy and Daddy, it will be very hard for you later to obey teachers, coaches, and bosses; even God Himself when He asks you to do something. God commands me in His Word to train you. Because you did not obey me, you will receive two spankings." Then, as you spank, in a calm voice count. "One. (spank), Two. (spank)." This is important to count because it helps you to stay calm and under complete control of yourself ensuring you do not discipline overly much, and the heart of your child understands exactly what she did and what the punishment is. Again, stay calm, and discipline in love. If you cannot stay calm and in control of your own anger, then you have no business spanking at that moment. When you are instructing your children or training them, keep your voice calm; otherwise, you will train your children to tune out unless your voice reaches a certain volume.

Too many kids I know disobey their parents, and then the worn-out parents waste a lot of unnecessary energy screaming at them, putting them down, and telling their kids things like, "You'll never do such and such" or "You'll always do..." But the parents absolutely fail at getting obedience. They just give up. The kids gets trained all right; trained to understand they don't need to obey their mothers when the only consequence is their mothers' tongues. (And incidentally, what do you think scars deeper in the long run?)

I can honestly tell you after three children we only very rarely needed to spank our children after the age of four. Maybe only twice that I can think of, and I believe it had to do with disrespect. Beyond age six, there was no more need to spank. By the time they were four, they obeyed us right away whatever we would ask. They were all three happy, healthy, well-adjusted kids. Consequently, my children recognized when they were around children who consistently disobeyed their parents or treated others with unkindness. Around three months ago, my eldest daughter Abigail came to me and said, "Thank you, Mom, for always having time for us, for sacrificing so many things to raise us, and training us to love God. I am grateful." What else can compare with that? She is a beautiful, well-adjusted, young woman ready to be a blessing to others and a great mother herself one day! She is a straight A student; varsity, cross-country runner; student council secretary; leader of Fellowship of Christian Athletes; and was voted homecoming queen to the glory of God. I say this not to brag, but to show you it's possible to raise Jesus-loving, pure, holy kids who are well-adjusted, well-liked, and hard working.

Before I close this chapter, I want to share a story of the hardest discipline I can ever remember administering. It goes along with the story at the beginning of the chapter. While our children were small, we were missionaries to the Wolof people in Senegal, West Africa. We lived near the edge of the Sahara Desert for language learning. We only had access to a very few ingredients of food to eat each day. Cooking was also quite difficult as our water was obtained on foot over a mile away, and what we cooked was over a small propane tank with one small flame. Every bit of cooking was a true labor of love. Basically, our only options were: fish, rice, oil, carrots, turnips, garlic, sweet potato, eggplant and a few greens such as parsley and mint. So, consequently, it was eat fish or waste away to nothing.

My three-year-old, Abigail, really did not like the strong taste of African food and did not want to eat her fish one day. She refused. I told her calmly if she refused to eat the fish, I would save it for dinner. At dinner, she refused to eat her meal again. I told her she would then be given the same choice for breakfast. I sent her to bed on an empty stomach. The next day I cheerfully presented her with the rice and fish dinner again. She refused to eat it. I told her calmly it was our best and only option. She needed to learn to eat it because not only was it good for her, but delicious. (It was.) Two more meals went by. Abigail dug her heels in and would not eat. Of course, I was giving her lots of water and keeping that fish and rice ever available.

Finally, on the third day a full six meals later she eagerly woke up and happily ate the entire plate of fish and rice! Guess what? For lunch that day she was presented with a fresh hot plate of fish and rice. Did she complain? Whine? NO! Not one more word was ever heard by our little girl about food. She was trained to eat whatever we set in front of her. Was it hard? You bet it was. I was checking on her constantly and worrying about her. But you know what? She looked fine! Best part? Guess what food my daughter loves now? You guessed it: African fish and rice. Bon Appetite!

CHAPTER 11

Leading Your Children to God

A ll three of our children have given their lives to the Lord at very young ages. I believe they were all three or four years old when it happened, and at least with Abigail, it happened as a direct result of consistent discipline, teaching, and training. I always viewed each time my children were rebellious as youngsters as an opportunity to tell them about the cross of Jesus. If they were walking in known disobedience (in other words, if they were old enough to know what they were doing, what was expected of them, and they failed to do it; it is sin), and I needed to pull them aside to bring correction or discipline of any sort, I always coupled it with a story about the beautiful love of Jesus. I reminded them how He died on the cross for them so they might be forgiven one-hundred percent and given the power to live holy lives.

My husband, as I said, has led many, many people to Jesus, but God in His mercy allowed me to be the one to lead our own three kids to Jesus. What a precious privilege! They have never been the same. Believe me when I tell you, you will know in your spirit when they understand and are ready for the repentance to give their lives to the Lord. The beautiful thing about motherhood is you have the rare opportunity to disciple your children before they even give their lives to the Lord. So by the time they do, they are already walking in much truth. Here is a little letter I wrote my then four-year-old daughter, Abigail, on the day she gave her life to Jesus.

One day, Abigail, I know you may want to have this testimony to read of how you came to a saving faith in Jesus since it happened for you as a very young child. Tonight, is August 13, 2003, and we are living in Dakar, Senegal. Two mornings ago during my own quiet time with Jesus, I asked the Holy Spirit to speak to me if there was anything He would like to tell me. Well, on that morning, I sensed He was saying to me I should pray for you to receive Him, and I should look for opportunities to share the gospel with you. You have only just recently turned four-years-old and I wondered if you were old enough to make such a decision. The Lord seemed to think so. You are already filled with the Word of God. Your daddy has been faithful to help you memorize the Word each day and you have a real capacity to understand things and articulate yourself well beyond your years.

Today was a particularly grueling day for you. We all seemed to be a bit hurried, grouchy, and in need of Jesus to help us. Daddy was getting ready to leave on a trip for a few days and your best little friends here in Dakar were getting ready to move far away. Caleb was going through a difficult stage of always wanting whatever you happened to have and so sometimes it ended up in fights between the two of you. Many times, today I had to help re-align you with a spanking to what God wanted you to be doing. We had some one-on-one time talking about how Jesus required you to be obedient and to honor me as your mommy.

This afternoon when you laid down for a nap and after daddy had left for his trip, I was all of a sudden overcome with the desire to pray for your soul. Abigail, I had a strong sense I was engaging in warfare for you and God was asking me to pray through it. I prayed for you to come to know Jesus, and I specifically asked God would draw you to Himself even today. Well, in the afternoon, Rachael and Kristen came by to play and you were not in the mood to play at all. All afternoon, you were not your usual cheerful and happy self to engage in play. Instead, you were really having a hard time even just functioning. Almost everything made you cry. I really think looking back you were like a little, spiritual barometer today, and the warfare was such you couldn't handle it.

Twice I called you to ask Jesus to come and help you. You did so both times; the second time you came with tears. After that, you honestly perked up and finally began to enjoy your friends. After they went home, Caleb and you were up to your usual nightly antics and I was getting you ready for bed when you both got the giggles. It had been a long day and I began

85

to dread the thought of it getting any longer. After praying, I decided to tell the story of Abraham while you both lay in your beds, side by side. Abigail, you were really listening. I then described how Abraham believed God and obediently followed Him to a land he had not yet seen. I told you the whole, long story right up to Isaac being offered and then God stepping in at the last minute to provide the ram. I told you how God promised Abraham his descendants would be as numerous as the stars in the sky. (At this point Caleb who I had thought was already asleep, started to shout, "Stars! Stars!") I said we were the children of Abraham, and those who follow Jesus. You wanted to know where Abraham was now, and I told you he was in Heaven with Jesus. You asked, "Will Grandma go there one day?" I said, "Yes." "And will Pop-pop go there too? What about Daddy and you?" you asked me. I told you we would all be there one day because we had all decided to invite Jesus to be our Lord. You said you wanted Jesus to be your Lord too. You wanted Jesus to come into your heart too. I asked you if you wanted to do that right now, and you said "yes!" Without hesitation you prayed a spontaneous prayer, "Jesus, please come into my heart."

Then I explained to you again how we were sinners in need of a Savior; how Jesus was our Savior who died for us and now He wanted to have a relationship with us for eternity to be with us in Heaven one day. You understood as much as you could. I honestly think with all my heart you had experienced a saving faith in Christ. I told you now the Holy Spirit lives inside of you and you are a part of God's special family. Abigail, I saw such a visible peace and joy, wash over your countenance and sensed a peace in my own spirit. You, my precious little four-year-old Abigail, were now a true daughter of the Highest King and wearing garments which were washed in the blood of the Lamb. You were my sister in Christ for all of eternity. How I praised God for working this miracle in your life at such a young, tender age, Sweetheart. You were going to see God do great things as you walked with Him each day. I prayed your faith and trust in the One who died for you would never dim or waiver. You would allow Jesus to lavish His perfect love upon you each day of your life.

May you never lack for hearing Him speak to you through His word and every time the Shepherd calls your name, Abigail, I pray you will promptly and obediently respond to Him out of a heart of love. I love you, Sweetie! Your daddy and I are thrilled with your choice to follow Jesus.

Love you always and always and always,
Your mommy

What a privilege to lead your own kids to Jesus. That letter was written thirteen years ago. Abigail has always loved the Lord since that day until now. We have never had a period of rebellion, and she has been a complete and total joy to watch and love. Around age thirteen, I remember Abigail having a stage where her faith was becoming her own. She was questioning, thinking deeply, and feeling differently than most kids her age, but she came through it. This season cemented her faith even stronger. I respect my daughter so much.

I now have a soon to be graduated daughter, a ninth grade son, and one fourth grader. I can honestly say I love each stage of parenting more and more and more. They are not perfect kids, and I am far from a perfect parent, but we truly do strive as a family to walk in unity and love for God and each other.

I have found in parenting through the teenage years it requires a lot more talking, praying together one-on-one, and listening. The temptations our teens face are incredible and we as moms need to be wise as serpents! In our home, we have not allowed our teens to have cell phones. We do not have any cable service. We never have. We feel these things are an unnecessary temptation and time suckers for teens whose brains and emotional makeup are still developing. We want our kids to find better ways of spending their time. They are all so busy anyway with sports, school, work, friends, and church. That is the way we like it. We are proud of who they are becoming and how they are choosing Jesus time and time again in their decisions. My son Caleb just told me this week he and his best friend just made a commitment to one another to never drink alcohol. I knew my son never would, but I think it is beautiful when I hear he is impacting his friend as well. He is getting ready to go on a mission's trip to Africa with Wade to preach 1 Timothy. I know it will be life changing and a powerful time shaping him into the man he is destined to become.

My daughter Abigail is finishing her senior year, and in spite of being beautiful, charming, and intelligent, she has never had a boyfriend. Why? She is choosing to wait for the one God has just for her. She has chosen the path of purity. Do you know statistics tell of America? Only five percent of women today make it to their wedding nights as virgins? Even if there is a greater number, let's say fifteen percent, this shows you the condition of our society. My daughter has determined in her heart and settled in her mind she will be one of those five percent. I honor her. She has expressed though sorrows if she will ever meet a guy who is doing the same thing. I pray constantly she will and he will be worth the wait. I trust God has good plans for her and for my boys. I trust there are other mothers and fathers out there committed to raising kids who walk in purity, holiness, love for God and for others. Kids who are willing to go against popular opinion and peer pressure to stand for Christ in their generation.

Are you one of those moms? I have a feeling you are, or you want to be! I pray with all my heart this short testimony and encouragement has given you hope. You are not alone. There are other mothers out there praying their hearts out and crying out for God to move and have His way with this next generation. God is with you even in your weakness and in the frailty or fickleness of your human love for Him. God hears your cry. He wants to meet you right where you are and fill you with His presence and love. He wants to give you the power to raise your kids to be incredible lovers of God. You can do it by His grace and even in your weakness as you lay yourself down. He will help and empower you. Are you ready? Let's go!

An Addition From my Daughter Abigail

Hi. I'm Abigail. I'm 17-years-old and am finishing my senior year in high school. I go to a small public high school in Hot Springs, South Dakota, but I desire to go to school at the International House of Prayer University in Kansas City, Missouri, after I graduate. I really want to go into missions of some kind after that, and the issue I feel God has laid on my heart specifically is sex trafficking which I'm sure you know is rampant all over the world. Sadly, it seems many governments and people in authority either turn pretty much a blind eye to it or just accept it. I desire to help people get out of that lifestyle and to learn to live in Christ!

Anyway, I just have a few things I trust God wants me to share that will be used in your lives. A few of the main things I want to emphasize are the importance of worship, reading God's Word, and God's love. As I begin, I just want to say I hope none of you reading this gets the impression I am a great, spiritual person. I am

91

far from where I want to be. I hope God will give me the grace to worship Him more as well as read and learn from His Word more.

Worshiping God is an extremely important way for us to give God the glory He so rightly deserves. One of the reasons I think God puts such a high level of importance on worship is because it is an act of the will. True, we can bring worship to God through the way we live our lives in accordance with His will, but the voluntary act of worship, actually speaking and singing out to God are things we must decide to do. I don't do this nearly as much as I should, but by God's grace I will grow. Did you know the Bible commands us over 300 times to "praise the Lord?" Just read the book of Psalms and try to count how many times that phrase is repeated! Worship, which is often simply declaring the attributes of God and what He has done, is also the best antidepressant. Seriously, think about it. When you start to feel depressed or discouraged, it is often because you're thinking primarily about yourself and your situation. Worship helps us get our eyes off our problems and ourselves. It helps us get them onto God and what He has done for us! It helps us to get an idea for the majesty and awesomeness of God! There is nothing sweeter than the knowledge God is still working in your life after you've felt He might have given up on you. His presence comes as the confirmation while you are worshiping. A sense of His never-failing love fills your heart, and you are filled with gratitude and love for Him as a response. I challenge you to try it! Next time you feel discouraged and down, just begin to worship God. You may not feel His presence right away, but as you continue to press into Him, He will come. As it says in Hebrews 11:6, the Lord is a rewarder of those who diligently seek Him.

I believe God uses worship together with His Word to renew our minds. As we read His Word, we should feel a sense of awe and a desire to worship God. Romans 12:2 says "...do not be conformed to this world, but be transformed by the renewing of your mind, that you may prove what is that good and acceptable and perfect will of God." How do we renew our minds? It's a hard thing with the garbage and filth coming at us from many directions. I attend public school, and the language I hear is often terrible. However, I have found when I have fixed my eyes on God and His pure Word, I have felt my mind literally being renewed. It's a great feeling and another reminder of how able and powerful God is to work on our behalf if we let Him. God's Word is such a blessing. Through it we gain knowledge of God and His character, how He feels about things and situations, how holy He is, and how much He loves us. To realize the God of the Old Testament is the same as Jesus Christ who provided a way for all people to be reconciled with Him through all history and eventually came to earth to provide a way of escape. This escape was through His own death and resurrection, even though our sin could have alienated us from Him forever. He gives us the gift of grace—grace leading to holiness! How awesome is our God! I challenge you to really read God's Word. Meditate on it, contemplate it, and think about it. You will feel God renewing your mind as you let His Word soak into you. Write a verse or two on a piece of paper and pull it out throughout the day to memorize it.

Imagine God is saying this to you right now...

I love you. I love you so much that I gave my Myself—
My Son—My life for you.

What will you do with that?

If you take it and run with it, you can have a life of joy

in Christ with an assurance of His unfailing, never fading love for you. Joy in the knowledge even if you should live isolated without a friend or another likeminded person around, you would still have a friend and companion of God. That's what He wants. Lovers of Himself. Those willing to love Him and His character so much they'd be willing to abide with Him. Leave all security and earthly comforts to run out with the One Who brings the greatest of comforts, companionship, and intimacy of fellowship with His friends. His love is so amazing! Love in the inside—deep, pure, like a well which will never run dry no matter how much you draw up. It remains level. A deep, cool, shadowy well of clear, calm water. Sometimes it can be hard to draw from a well; sometimes not so much. But when you're thirsty, it's worth it. His love changes everything and anything. In John 7:37-38, Jesus is speaking, and He says, "If anyone thirsts, let him come to Me and drink. He who believes in me, as the Scripture has said, out of His heart shall flow rivers of living water." When you are filled with the love of God, it overflows to others and gives you opportunities to share about Christ with them. In John 4:13-14, Jesus said, "Whoever drinks of this water will thirst again, but whoever drinks of the water that I shall give him will never thirst. But the water that I shall give him will become in him a fountain of water springing up into everlasting life."

I am challenged by the words of 1 Corinthians 13, which as many of you know is known as the "love chapter." Its main emphasis is how useless any efforts we make to do things for God in our own strength are without love. I can tend to feel I can do great things for God without being filled with Himself and with His love for people. Even things we do which have an outward form of love, but which we do without real love are pointless.

1 Corinthians 13:1-3 states,

Though I speak with the tongues of men and of angels, but have not love, I have become sounding brass or a clanging cymbal. And though I have the gift of prophecy, and understand all mysteries and all knowledge, and though I have all faith, so that I could remove mountains, but have not love, I am nothing. And though I bestow all my goods to feed the poor, and though I give my body to be burned, but have not love, it profits me nothing. (Emphasis mine)

In God's eyes, even our actions however righteous-seeming they may be, are nothing without love. Only love can motivate someone to truly have a lasting impact for Christ. It's easy enough to be called to be a missionary and even stick it out for a while. Giving all you have to feed the poor or even die for Christ, but to *live* with the kind of love Christ had for us and expend ourselves for the sake of others coming to know Christ is an entirely different matter.

I challenge you to try to live with love for everyone you encounter. You'll never know what battles others are fighting. How would Jesus make people feel? Loved! Accepted! Understood! Wanted! There are times to speak the hard truth in love, and if you ask Him, God will give you the wisdom to know when.

Identity in Christ

Another thing I think very important to know is our identity should not be found in the world or in what people say about us, but in what God says about us So many people, Christians as well as unbelievers, struggle with identity issues. I see many girls my age who put their whole identity in what their boyfriend (or ex-boyfriend) says about them. I personally think this is a bit ridiculous. I have chosen not to date until the one guy who I feel like I could marry comes along. If God wants me to get married, great! He'll provide someone who is even stronger and farther along in their walk with Him than I am. Someone like-minded who I can respect. But if God doesn't want me to marry, great! I can serve Jesus on my own and with like-minded friends. My identity is not wrapped up in what some man says about me. My identity is not found in what my parents or friends say about me. My identity is not found in how many "likes" or comments I get on a Facebook post. My identity, when all is said and done, is found in where I stand in God.

Did God send His only Son to die for me? Yes! Does God love me? Yes! Does God care for me? Yes! Does God call me His child? Yes! Is God's opinion the only one that matters? Yes!

Let your identity be found in Christ. Your circumstances do not define you. What defines you is whether or not you are a child of God walking in His plan for your life.

NEED ADDITIONAL COPIES?

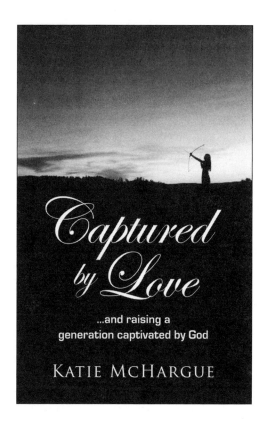

To order more copies of

Captured by Love

contact CertaPublishing.com

- ❑ Order online at:

  www.CertaPublishing/CapturedByLove

- ❑ Call 855-77-CERTA or

- ❑ Email Info@CertaPublishing.com